BROTHER TO DRAGONS, COMPANION TO OWLS

BROTHER TO DRAGONS,

COMPANION TO OWLS

SERAPHIM EDITIONS
2004

The publisher gratefully acknowledges the financial assistance of
the Canada Council for the Arts.

Canada Council   Conseil des Arts
    for the Arts   du Canada

Published in 2004 by
Seraphim Editions
238 Emerald Street North
Hamilton, Ontario
Canada L8L 5K8
www.seraphimeditions.com

NATIONAL LIBRARY OF CANADA CATALOGUING IN PUBLICATION

Jarmai, Andrea
    Brother to dragons, companion to owls / Andrea Jarmai.

Poems.
ISBN 0-9734588-1-X

    I. Title.

PS8569.A597B76 2004   C811'.6   C2003-907345-9

EDITOR: Allan Briesmaster
COVER ENGRAVING: "History" by Eric Gill (1934)
AUTHOR PHOTO: V. Tony Hauser
DESIGN: Carleton Wilson

Printed in Canada

METROPOLIS

This is the meeting place.
The waters flow round Toronto Island
and lap at the feet of the city,
mirror the faces of long ago people,
cultures that pass and repass here.
The lake draws the skyline, bends
it inside the camera's glass eye.
Calm surface-ripples round out
the corners. No angles in nature,
straight lines in space.

Her steps are iambic, she's
limping a little and murmurs
a thank you, a blessing along
the length of Queen West, one hand
a bit forward, with a few quarters
held in a cup. She's squamous
and grateful, her smile genuine.
This, too, is a living, at least,
and it is spring.

The heart of a city – where does it
beat? Above, on the streets, or deep under-
ground, in the subway arteries? Her feet
lag, the smile still appears
apprehensive as she watches the horsemen
dismount. In their sinking clepsydral bowls
she pours her cupped earnings, feeds
and waters the horses – this is
the meeting place.

Wind shudders the lake,
once more the bowl rises. The sun
peels golden skin off the Royal
Bank Plaza, gilds the glass

cathedral of BCE Place. Power-
tie, briefcase, a new VP takes
the escalator, beating the clepsydra
down. His time is five figures plus
a sales incentive – what's that in quarters?
Yet, his heart's in the right place,
he really does love his neighbour, he just
doesn't know where she lives. He
drives a black Saab, horsemen are no
match for him.

Spinning the wheels of all his nine
lives, as the bowl rises again
over Nathan Phillips Square, a Young
Prince comes curb-leaping back-
wards, flashing his flame-
coloured skateboard, the spring
in his grin and his don't give a flying
attitude. Here is heart
enough for two megacities
iambically beating the rush-hour
traffic, he only just misses her, wild
horsemen couldn't catch him
today.

Why does the heart,
the great pumping heart of the city
not burst apart in the spring?
The joy, the pain, the grief, the
indifference of it – how is it the lake
does not boil, overwhelm in one great,
ventricular heave its topless towers?
She holds out her cup, bids us
drink, us and the horsemen. Who
can drain it? She whispers, "Young Prince,
or you, powerful VP, come, wrestle me."

Her cup is a horn, its end in the lake,
she is Old Age whom Thor himself
could not conquer. The young blades strain,
swallow; the lake recedes. The four
horses drink on in the twilight.

Night falls. The seals still
unbroken, over the great clepsydra
of the Hydro building there is reflective
silence. Far away, in the cave of the winds,
four horses are tied, reins
hung on a tree. A pale dawn
rises above the city, another
morning. This is the place
of meeting.

CATHEDRAL

In the living cathedral
the sun streams slantwise
through stained-glass petals
of a myriad orchids'
translucent flesh;
a mesh of green fire
in the cathedral windows
of the rain forest.

Great Gothic boles, towering cedars,
dark Doric oaks, slender
Corinthian umbrella trees anchor
vines, liana-hung apses;
calyx thuribles heavily swinging
from long nodding stalks,
frankincense slowly exhaling
ozone. Breathe.

Chants, incantations
of great golden bees, throngs
of insects, the whirr
of ruby-throated wings:
congregations of iridescent angels
hovering emerald, gleaming metallic
in specks of dust swirling
through sunshafts along the nave.

A single orchid –
one perfect orchid – opens
its true heart, pure soul exposed,
mortal part burnt away –
golden wings beating
above the loam ashes
on the living altar
of great Paracelsus' dreams.

ICARUS

for W.H. Auden

The AGO is just round the corner.
No figure of speech, this, it is true;
that's why we live here.
Once a week or so, if I can,
I drop in for a moment to see
a favourite painting, say hello
to a beloved sculpture, often the same
as the week before, or the week
before that. We have an understanding.
Foul or fair, I come to visit;
they are there, waiting.

Rushing in at the end of a rainy day,
I drop the umbrella off at the coat-
check, pass the guard at the entrance, and
cross the Rotunda. From there I can see
him, keeping lookout for me.
Van Dyke's Icarus, wings just unfolding.
That heady moment when all is still
possible; man achieves flight, before
the sun-rise, the light, death
in the ocean.

The eyes that look at me, questioning,
are meant for Daedalus; father,
magician, his strong right hand
pointing silently upward; the boy's –
uncertain – down. It is the Buddha's
gesture: "Between heaven and earth
there is only I." The face is wistful,
trusting. Very young.

And I wonder,
always, as I stand before him,
our eyes locked: which of us
got it right? He, in the heavens,
dead of his passion, or I, here,
feet on the ground, alive.

And I know, as I always know,
next week I'll return. I see in his eyes
he will try it again, if I'm not here
to ground him. When I am not there,
holding him to it, is he still waiting,
wings safely folded, keeping his word?

LABYRINTH

In her small hut
on sea-girt Naxos
mad old Ariadne dreams.
Nights go by slowly;
the golden thread lost,
the dreams move in circles.
Sometimes she raves.
Daylight is easier,
the local farmers are kind.
On slaughtering days
they allow her to garland
the calves she calls brothers;
when she weeps
they lead her gently away.
The children bring honeycombs,
the women plait flowers
into her thinning hair –
lest the gods envy beauty
they've hidden her mirror
some time ago.
On every new daisy
the last-plucked petal
ends in "he loves me;"
the annual mail-boat
still brings a message,
"Coming in spring."
The words are simple,
the dialect local,
but madness is merciful
in some ways.
On sea-girt Naxos
the seasons go by,
no-one keeps count.
The year circles,
and begins again.

Divina Commedia dell'Arte

for David, 20 January 2002

On Sunday it rained
apples and oranges
and the Lord came among us
(passo suave)
as we stood singing
Mass and Marriage
(a one and a two)
a slim, slippery Harlequin
*(garçon fatal, he catered
the wine and the food)*
juggling apples and oranges
(a one and a two and so on)
with a horizon grin
and a rainbow-shift
sun-sequined suit.
And the questions he asked us
were multiple, choice,
and the answers to all were
True.

So came it that You,
Adonai, at last
were unmasked,
(Sir)
a slip of a Jester in bells,
Magician in motley,
(party jongleur)
Narcissist child who in dark
and dark
had rocked and echoed
Himself – the only
love He knew –
re-echoed Himself as Such
and Such
*(such apples as I,
such oranges as you)*
dropping nary a one
nor a two.

VIDE COR MEUM

for David, first anniversary

My heart beats like Dante's
in the half-light the Greeks called
Lykophoros – wolf-light –
of morning before waking,
before the taking
of vows, when promises
unmade as yet
have their birth in the
glow of the half-closed eye.

My heart beats like Dante's
when Beatrice walks
by the Arno in half-light
at vespers, before saying
her evening prayers, when vows
never made, yet kept forever
come out with the stars
in the Florentine half-light
burning black holes
into the night.

My heart beats like Dante's
in the half-light, the wolf-light
of morning, waking beside you,
walking to work, taking
the streetcar when it is cold,
my hand in your pocket
growing warm, growing older
in heaven or hell, or
the place inbetween them:
somewhere in that half-light
I know Dante's heart.

Juliet

She came in violet heaves over scarlet
wine shot in Tantalus' maddened blood,
asked not, nor spoke, gave no quarter, no sign,
just sat on my left.
I thought it was God.

She came like religion, in strings of hope,
in tomorrows, in drugs, in dreams, in stars,
in roses, in thorns, in knife-wounds, in sutures,
in bruises, in healing,
in kissed-over scars.

She died as a star dies, light-years away,
one silent downward-curving arc;
as suns die, exploding without a sound
inside a telescope
during the night.

Night Vision

Titanic, 15 April 1912

The dreams
are coloured
I know
many in blue
those
of yesterday
tonight's
in black
and those
of tomorrow
below
the Atlantic
the sky
looks like
the outer
space
I've never
seen
we did not go
there in my day
where the dreams
come from
I cannot tell
so cold
in the water
thinking
is slow
it's just as well
you're holding
my hand
otherwise I might
be afraid
I heard

someone singing
just then
and it may
be true
we're nearer
to God but
here in the dark
my love
in the end I'm
nearest to you

Valentine on the 20th Floor

for David, St. Valentine's Day 2002

Up here
I feel the city surge
beneath us
like the ocean-swell heaving
thousands of fathoms
below thinning spring sheet-ice –
vestigial skin –
under an Antarctic tent.

Up here
in this glass tower,
too high for temptation,
we cast no stones.
For evil weighs
like smashed lead crystal,
and is worth its weight
in silver pieces
caught in a cup
by the Arimathean
long ago.

Up here
on Mont Salvat
we guard the Grail.
Twisted diamonds
encrust the panes
of February.
Our horizon is blinded,
ice reflects inward;
I see only you.

On the stereo
a late Haydn symphony
sounds like early Mozart;
late winter,
up here with you,
like early spring.

Holy Hour, Midnight

First Friday in March, in cell, bed- and barroom.
The night falls with the veils and wassails.
Each keeps the vigil. At St. Michael's Alehouse
the goblets tilt, the violin wails,

and up at the convent, in pristine cold whiteness,
nuns waltz in pairs to a shy Father's song,
waking echoes of that imperfect Eden
mislaid for heaven. Memory is long.

The Grail and the Pendulum

for Joseph Campbell, with thanks

The land was always blighted.
From Logres to Los Angeles,
little change, but this:
the King.

Who, now, is the Fisher?
Heal the wound, restore the land:
the prize, the quest, the game
was ever, then and still, the same.

We've torn away the masks of God
till all that's left are mirrors. By now,
we've gazed our fill. The work
begins again.

What we need is a hero. One
among a thousand faces sharp
enough to know a King, and dumb
enough to ask no questions.

Find a cup that's big enough
to hold and heal and patch
all the holes we've dug –
this time, in the ozone layer.

Cancer; AIDS; dioxin; landfills;
Chernobyl and such –
a plague
by any name –

Dare we crack the mirror? Lest
seven years bad luck –
seven years of Pharaoh's dream –
withered corn and stricken kine –

put our faces at low ebb
in a bell-curved universe
without a Joseph?
A Moses to lead us out?

What we need is a hero. Wagner's
digitally remastered
hesitant prizefighter:
Neo-Parsifal.

The land was always blighted,
only the poison's new. The rules,
the basic truths, remain the same:
we start, advance, and lose –

spring, summer, autumn – then,
the Moderator's call.
En route lies the choice, the Quest
for where to take it all.

The Pendulum swings
round one fixed point. From
Camlann field to Umm Qasar; Lidice
to Moscow; what's new in Beijing?

From Wasteland circling Carbonek
to rainforest round Rio,
the land was always blighted.
It is blighted still.

Little changes but the latest
fashions, technical advances,
that screw around
with constants.

Plain as π and
simple mathematics: what
we need is a hero.
24   And a King.

GEODE

In a cluttered junkshop it surfaced
again. The tag said "rock crystal," a small,
dark cave. Microcosm, she thought;
and bought it for memory's sake.
That night she stared at flickering rainbows
thrown by the candle near the bed
she'd set it beside; from the pillow
she could see up into its heart.

                              So small
this half-shell sits, snug for one hand;
the stone bark is grey, common stone,
but some fire smoulders, still, at the dark core:
the crystal keep where deep magic holds
the spell-bound avatar.

                        Prophecy
stirs; a sparrowhawk's shadow
falls on the pillow, the head that forgot
to blow out the flame before drifting to sleep.
Closed eyes recall in flashing sparks
struck from crystal the cave
where Merlin lies tombed, waiting
for someone to do the impossible,
draw the sword from the stone again;
call up the rainbow and believe that hell
has no fury here, Nimuë no power;
the light cast by the candle
of a dreaming woman can, for a while,
just while the dream lasts,
break any spell.

WOMAN AS MOUNTAIN

Look at me, Gilgamesh.
I am Humbaba, Humbabuschka,
a ten on the Richter scale,
but only for you.

Come to me, Gilgamesh.
I am yours only.
Climb my hills, enter
my caves, deep forests.
Explore me.

> *Make your name: plant your flag,*
> *take photographs. Tell everyone*
> *you were the first, that*
> *you named me.*

I am immense, dangerous;
the widow mountain.
Gilgamesh, love me.

One day they will find you
face down on my shoulder,
frozen skin snow white, fit
monument in cold alabaster –
like forgotten Mallory –
and the papers will speculate if,
when you died,
you were on your way up,
which does not count, or
on your way down,
and triumphant.

PIETÁ

for Jean Hull Herman

Come closer, Mary, lean over
my shoulder. Let us dream a while
in the golden afternoon of summer.
The oak tree's shade has made me drowsy,
Pia; let the dark tent of your hair descend
like the night over Chaldéa.

The sky perceptibly darkening,
the huge wings slicing through the calm
of that other afternoon when you
alone in the courtyard felt the earth
move inside your head, as Gabriel, descending,
called you blessed. And you, whose maidenhead
would polarize the ages east to west
in two schools quarrelling,
whom harsh women would hold up as
the servile scapegoat of a gray philosophy,
stood the angel's fiery glance, assenting
to the task none else would have the heart
to undertake. When the wingbeats ceased
and the sun returned, with the stunned
birds in their trees still silent, paralysed,
you threw your head back, staring long
and straight into the sun
and turned thence inward to be dazzled
by the thing within. Your breast
contains what no human creature could
look at straight and not be blinded. Lest
so much light should lead to pride and kill
the very thing it would give birth to,
you veil it in the deep blue of the ocean,
white of the morning star, the lily,
and the honeybee's golden homespun.

Let me lay my head, Mary, on your breast,
let me breathe the lily fragrance

of your dress. Let me rest upon your heart
and dream this golden afternoon. Lean over me,
Pia, let the dark tent of your hair descend
like the night over Chaldéa.

CHI: BLOOD AND EARTH

(Mishima Yukio)

He carried his blood like a signature
that he was the last of his kind.
When he knew it for certain
he died.

The flesh is the earth the blood runs heir to;
we choose to break or to bend.
Or neither. He chose
to stand.

Astride the gap between art and life,
the question of might for the pen or the sword
he put to the test
and solved.

He wielded both as merely twin edges
of a single covenant: the Mind.
He wrote his own contract.
And signed.

CLERIHEWN INTERVIEW: REVIEW

Harbourfront Festival of Authors, 24 October 2002

John Polanyi
had only a tiny
condenser mike: a little sparrow perched tight
on his jacket-lapel that Thursday night.

Umberto Eco
had a similar micro-
microphone. Miracles, really, these little birds,
to carry the weight of such winged words.

JEAN-LOUIS BARRAULT

Trapped in two dimensions on an empty stage,
defining his space by the span of his arms,
he summoned the third by tacit command
for air to solidify.

Artistic medium: Motion on void.
Form: Four-dimensional figure.
Time: Heartbeat-iambic.
Title: Mime.

The Mad Hatter dances and holds my hand,
drags me up and down a dreary chessboard land;
pawns to the left of me and pawns to the right,
pawns to the front and rear – and not a king in sight.

The Mad Hatter keeps on exchanging my hat:
I turn into Queen, Duchess, grinning Cheshire Cat.
"Please, I am Alice, Sir!" I try my best to scream,
but the hats keep flowing in an endless stream.

"A thousand hats or a thousand masks –
what might be the difference?" the Hatter asks.
"If the hats all fit, you get to wear them all,
be the Queen of all the pawns, and ten feet tall."

"I don't want the pawns, and the hats hurt my head;
the masks are too heavy – they weigh me down like lead;
since there's miles and miles of this black-and-white-
    checked sand,
there must be a King to rule this chessboard land!"

The Mad Hatter laughs: "Can't you see the light?
These fields have an end and there's a King, all right,
but you won't find him; and even if you do,
with all those hats about, he won't know it's you."

Mongol Horse

Shotsprung from thunderside of godspeed
Earthfashion clayflesh nurtured to skysoul
Sinews at bowstretch, nostrils to windflare
Chessmanshort brushmane archbent to breakneck
Hoofhammer heartbeat dustwhirl away.

Legroom for homeground, bloodstream to boilstir
Skinsparkle sweatcoat catchfire fulltilt
Flashburst on barren tundra of sunbake
Thundercross headlong drumtaut horizon
Flatliner silence deadfall in wake.

Mikisi

for the Bald Eagle Mikisi at the Metro Toronto Zoo

You are the enigma, low
hard-eyed form of an estranged immortal,
mad Sweeney from the battle of Moira
sharing forever Icarus' longing
to breast the shivering current
on the jagged edges of sunrise,
above the Napoleons of mirage.

No crimson violence here, my purple
passager. No knifepoint plummets
to strike at the heart in flight: prisoner,
safe here, expiating at the waste forest's
centre, on the ashes and sackcloth
of an ascetic demi-paradise.

I, guest in the Grail castle, pale
beneath the fool's ill-fitting red armour,
dumbstruck, exalted, ask no questions;
you in your sovereign innocence,
unwittingly beloved like the poet
or the whore, suffer the stroking hand
in grace oblivious as lilies.

On our stage the speaking parts
are cast in different tongues – in a glass
darkly, marking time. If we speak
at all, we go through the motions
as mime to platonic mime.

The Hero Says No

Parsifal On Mont Salvat Reconsiders His Mythological Archetype

I am Beauty in worlds that boast no Beast,
a Jedi without an Empire to fight.
Mocked up in homespun, some call me a fool,
and maybe I am, armed like a knight.

Shy of the truth, I am the guardian of silence,
eternal crucible of not yets, not quites,
catspaw of illusion, scapegoat of reality,
memoryless messiah with introvert eyes.

My blindness is often mistaken for visions;
my visions are always taken for lies;
a voice like Cassandra's can't invite questions
regarding wherefores, whithers and whys.

I know I should ask concerning the Grail,
am aware I could save, being sure of my might;
I simply don't want to. I'm not really startled;
the lance is bleeding, but I'm used to that sight.

I shan't, while I admit that I really ought to,
yes, I *could* deliver the land from its blight.
It's pleasant to sojourn, though time be borrowed,
here in the garden of earthly delights.

The Puppet Master

Come in, sit down, come one, come all,
my puppets are at your beck and call.
See dragons, see princes, the King of the Mice,
see fools, see yourself, it's cheap at the price.

I pull the strings and the puppets dance.
They laugh, they cry, retreat, advance;
enter our world, forget who you are;
inside this theatre you'll feel like a star.

You'll love my puppets, they look so real,
carved with such skill, you'd swear they can feel.
There's almost a heartbeat: while I move the string
the inert wood is a living thing.

Lose yourselves in the puppets' games,
forget your cares, you can change your names,
be heroes, lovers, minstrels, queens;
these strings can grant you all your dreams.

You need do nothing, I'll sing the song:
he who does nothing can do no wrong,
who does no wrong need have no fear:
I'll take the risks, I'm the puppeteer.

Come in, sit down, come one, come all.
I've magic to charm the body and soul.
No worries, no doubts, whatever life brings,
it's cheap at the price: just give me your strings.

LUCIFER SPEAKS

after Raymond Queneau

Knowledge, of a sort, is what I was after,
some militant spark to salvage a life
of mindless perfection as chartered lamplighter
in an absence of night; little bureaucrat,
with a job in name only, appointed to save
his face in the mirror, gaudy image
of the dumb blond archangel caught
in the glass lit by his proper heavenly
body exuding the useless, redundant
radiance each morning reborn.

I looked for what would render in substance
the empty placebo, impotent symbol
of my name – "Come in, my angel,
first among seconds, rise from the gutter.
I, your creator, will make you a star . . ."
I wanted some reason for not being elsewhere;
a career, if you will, to banish the boredom,
the jaded inertia that absolute good
imparts to unsullied virtue; to find
something raw, rediscover the taste
of our daily ambrosia, flung to us without fail
every heavenly thrice-blessed day.
I wanted it all. Lordship; choices;
knowledge my brain presupposed.
Like the image template, I am that I am –
no puppet of clay.

Beauty, of a sort, is what I was after,
and sure knowledge that it was indeed my truth;
Lucifer, judging with power of veto
all I've created; with certain vision
and practised hand, see and say:

"This is good!" What matters good in this
unquesting utopia where Good Triumphant
shepherds our collective mind? I wanted
to take, not be given, what's mine. To worship?
Possibly; but not for a living. By choice,
open eyes levelled, perhaps at the throne,
perhaps at the mirror; render only
to God, not his creature, and not on my knees.

As lord of this place, I rule. The sulphur
blisters my skin; lurid by gaslight,
livid and scaly – thin; flame
sears my brain that raped the forbidden
tree of the exclusive – I burn. Scream
into the void, spew my frustration's
bilious venom into the Face of Gold
I once had loved, again and again:
I turn gold into lead, bring darkness full
circle for new light to spring, and arise golden:
pinioned phoenix on newly grown wings.

But what is the use; the sulphur clings,
Hellfire marks me its own –
here forever . . .
if Truth be Knowledge, it has not set me free.
Arms of Prometheus held out to the universe,
here I stand: Devil.

THE BARGAIN

Come in. Yes, I know you, it's not unexpected;
by invitation, as per the code.
The pleasure is mine. Do take a seat,
you prefer the fireside, I know.
May I get you a drink? Well, there's Glenlivet –
liquid fire, quite so.

I suppose I have that Faustian air,
why else this honour? Indeed, yes,
the rules are straightforward, I've read
the small print at the bottom, no fear.
My soul, in exchange for whatever I ask;
a princely offer, and fair.

But Faust was a lightweight, a poor
example; it's not that easy, you see.
Immortality, youth, fortune and glory –
these things are trifles. My price is your soul.
My soul for yours is readily bargained:
an eye for an eye. By the Book, on the whole.

It seems to me you're not rightly treated –
the whole game is rigged, it wasn't just you –
you offered the apple take it or leave it,
we netted hope when you took the fall.
But what of me, you ask. I'll take my chances;
it's reckoning time, that is all.

With my soul in hand, you've a passport; and I,
with my last act this mercy, may still qualify.
If not, I'll make do in the celestial basement;
poetic justice; I might have the call.
With so many saved, none of us perfect,
how are you different? A soul for a soul.

FAIRYTALE

after Stevie Smith

I got lost in a wood
and fell in a bog
I sat down and cried
and up came a frog

He gave me berries
and red red wine
and I was all his
and he was all mine

We danced and we sang
and we danced again
and late in the evening
I guessed his name

Now I'm pumpkins all over
and I've lost one shoe
I'm home safe in bed
and there's nothing to do

PIED PIPER

Were we so different,
all said and done,
marching in line to a
different drum?
Were we so hungry
not to be you,
every new tune worth
dancing, and true?
Was that road really
less travelled on,
or was it merely
farther from home?

Are we so humdrum
now we discern
one quiet bass beat
pulsing unheard
through the cacophony,
close to the earth;
each one iambic,
each one unique:
beat of my heart,
road at my feet.

SEA LEGENDS

The night still brings
in cold ocean silence

        farewell

the selkie's heartbeat
rising, falling

        failing

in hope
heliotrope of the far horizon
naked

awaiting redemption
sealed up
in our skins

        here

inhuman bodies
glistening, lissom
obeying

the eerie creak of timbers
groaning
the hull of the *Endurance*

drifting, vision blurring

on lone Elephant Island

souls in training
enduring, waiting

grim survivors
sealed away
beyond the pale

reach out in visions
glide beneath
some savage

        semi-conscious
        urge
        to bark.

The Ahab Cycle

in memoriam Gwendolyn MacEwen

1. *I, Ahab*

With this iron I do thee wed.
There are ropes attached, mind;
what hate has joined in one thrust
indifference on one part
won't soon put asunder
the bond.
I know no impediment to love in fire and thunder:
I kiss; consume now what you left me
the last time we met.
On this Manila cable,
the widow's son, sworn to go
on pain of dismembered'immolay to the end
of his tow; below; and there perish thought.
Perdition be damned, and so too Ahab – the arm
of the law, with one leg to stand on –
biblical authority – I come; a blow for a blow.
Pitiless Titans, feasting on kindred, we both;
the sin mine alone; because
I know.
I have heard the mermaids screaming
on Sirius' invisible shores:
"No more, thou cannibal, marked Zoroastrian,
lightning-struck Cain;
Nommo!"
Oh yes, they will scream for me.
Hot oil-blood poured in the ear of my half-shell,
that font,
spermaceti of kings, I'll own;
we deaf hear the ocean,
hear it roar, hear it roll, hear it call us all Ishmael
(dispossessed children of the lesser part of God,
the smaller ball),

as you all hear it in a conch placed adjacent,
but – I quote the raven: *that's all.*
I hear; I obey; I go;
where no man must go before me,
virgin white Kali; I go.
To die; to sleep;
perchance to know.

II. *Ahab in Love*

You know, they say he hated that whale,
and hunted it just for revenge. Well, hey,
if he saw it as male, that might be so,
but me, I say,
he talks to it, hates it,
like one hates a woman,
like one harps away
(and makes sure it stays harped,
goes with it, just in case)
at a thing that's already said nay.

III. *Judas' Dream*

Call me Ishmael.
Call me Cain –
brother to dragons,
companion to owls –
if you call me at all.

Call me now,
call me; take me . . .

Call me Pilate,
or Macbeth's lady;
wash my hands,
wash my feet, Mary . . .

if only
if only

poppy and memory

out of my depth, *O*
de profundis –

there is not enough water here;
there is not enough water
at all.

iv. *Whales Weep Not*

Whales weep not
over spilt drops
only
drops in the ocean
sparkling
rainbow-hued oil slicks
honey
oozing out slowly
through silvery pipes
milky
mother-of-pearl spills
whales weep not
it is the ocean leaking

v. *Call Me*

All roads lead down to water;
finally,
to the sea.
All roads run down, run out,
eventually . . .

Follow me,

he said. Seek,
and you shall find; or so
they say. Knock,
and a door shall be opened
to you (but not to me); ask,
and you shall be answered. Oh,
were it so easy!
All roads may lead to water,
but not all may drink.
I know.

Seek I did; found I had
shipped with Ahab, away
from every door but one:
this coffin lid I float on – now –
still it is closed, to me;
will not let in the sea:
liferaft, barrier, preserver against
a sea of answers to questions that I asked,
too; along with Ahab. Who knows –
for whom it opened. Opened and swallowed
all. All but one.

When shall my soul be required of me?
When the sea shall give up its dead,
will it then beckon,
will it give up the answer
on that Day? To me?

Call me Ishmael; call me now;
by any other name; by your own;
call me anything, call me anywhere,
but call!
And take me. Take me there.
Dispossessed by father;
even by the Father
of all – of all on board alone
rejected – finally,
even
by the sea.

VI. *Fishing with Ahab*

Killifish big
Killifish white
Killifish come
Feel Ahab's pike
Killifish where ticklish?
Here, in the heart?
Here Killy, here Killy
Let me kill'ee
If Ahab can't killy
Killy kill me.

VII. *Ahab Asleep – in Ophelia's Garden*

Here is datura. That's to take you
where few would go willingly.
And here –
mandragora. That's to make it
easier to swallow. You know.
Now go.
And when you get there,
they'll open your mouth
with a sharp little knife
and they'll weigh your heart
against the feather of Maat,
and what, then,
Ahab, my brother,
Ahab, my Other,
will you say?
That your love for the whale
grew every day;
that you always loved most
those who came
to destroy you?

　　Heart and feather
　　suspended forever . . .

Mein fliegende Holländer,
I will fill up your grail
with poppy and memory;
you will trust your ship to me.

I will hoist your sail wide,
billowing, white,
a skirt, a swan, a whale –
a wedding gown
to love and devour in,
surrender and drown in –

I will raise the white feather of Maat
and plunge it into your heart –
we both know the truth
can kill.

AKHENATEN

for Daniel Kolos

Moving on these burial walls,
two-dimensional, immortal,
you navigate the night-path
of your sire-self, the sun.
Rays that end in hands
hold, fold your body's grotesque –
the rounded hips, swollen thighs,
Oedipus-legs and long, strange eyes
(though not yet blinded),
stung lips of the honey-thief
branded, beloved of bees.

Non omnis moriar.
Introibo ad altare Dei.

Marriage bed – the thorns
your own devising – where
your winged mother bled
and fed you honey, stolen, royal,
jelly for the King (for once),
stung your lips to pillows – oh!
the dance she led you
on that flight of flights
to possess the Queen of All!
She, orchid calyx, open,
you, metallic orchid-bee,
golden scarab rolling such
(and nonesuch) little balls of clay.
Together you gave birth to so much
more than just a little girl!

Non omnis moriar.

You shall not altogether die.
They will dip your limbs in honey-nectar,

49

forty days in siccant natron,
wind your swollen thighs in linen
(tight, beloved, oh so tight
the orchids under you will wither
in the rainforest of Egypt:
in the desert no bee
ever pollinates)

Introibo ad altare Dei.

Run. Run up these walls
along the shafts of sunlight hands
ascend,
ascend and tell him
you are desert, broken,
you are his,
that he should not have spoken
his unspeakable, blinding name
in your naked mind that day;
tell him he must find the knife,
split the pillows of your lips
open for the test of Maat;
let the poisoned honey drain
like feathers, drain,
like fetters . . .
stand transfixed, caressed,
transfigured
by shafts that end in hands and touch you –
touch you here . . . and here . . . – create
your self in truth and struggle
upon the altar-bed,
burst your thighs, legs, lips, your seed
the sun will germinate.

Non omnis moriar.

Descend.

Worship

I met a pilgrim in my halcyon days,
in his native land and mine, near the sea;
he held some marvellous flowers in his arms,
gently and carefully, like some precious thing.
They were for God, he said when I asked,
to lay on his altar in homage, when found,
the pick of his garden, with roots in his heart,
in God's house alone could their like survive,
it is there he was bound.

I met him again in my middle years,
with the same flowers, but in another land.
The flowers had withered, and he held them low,
his eyes were haunted, and his face was gaunt.
Priests he had found in their pallid towers,
temples and churches, but none of God's grace;
their fairest vessels could not hold his flowers,
the quest was yet on, for some other altar,
some other place.

We met for the last time under desert sun.
He'd dried like his flowers, his skin was scored,
but his eyes were clear, the haunted look gone,
and he bore his withered bouquet like a sword.
Yes he said, they were still the same, it is he
who had changed; he had held God's hand,
and knelt at His altar. When I asked him where,
I think he smiled. And with loving care
laid his flowers on the sand.

You, My God

You called, I thought, and I came running,
heedless of all the hurt
you'd caused with former silence,
when I stood here forgetting wisdom,
the seven-pillared worthy house
a maze,
and clutched at my dead heroes,
seeing your face
where my thoughts touched theirs.

But now I heard you call, and I have come,
you ask that I forsake
these wretched pagan shades
that kept me sane when your lips were cold,
when their love kept me from growing old.
You call me to your mansions where
there is no room for such as they.
Must you be won with pain?

Still, I came.

MICHELANGELO'S LAST PRAYER

from the Hungarian of George Faludy

Your anvil is the earth, and with your right arm
You span the arc of heaven like the sun.
Eight decades on this scaffolding – a lifetime –
I sought a sign of you, but there was none.

Under my chisel marble fell to stonedust,
But only torsos, idols would be born.
I found you not, elusive, radiant sunburst,
Who glowed there pulsing under every stone.

I have myself become an ancient stone block,
Split by vines, a still, curmudgeonly old rock,
But in my soul the old flame yet burns on.

How can I shed this flesh that holds me prisoner?
Strike me, if you can love a hoary sinner,
Divine Sculptor, My God. I am the stone.

THE PRINCE'S BALL

The lights were bright to blinding:
music eddied through wine,
azures and crimsons were dancing,
velvets and satins swayed time.

The eve of a birth or a marriage –
did somebody whisper "make a wish?"
Was it only the curtain that fell in the carriage
in a soft velvet swish?

And after . . . and after . . . that murmur . . .
was anyone really there?
Was there an indrawn breath, or
had one foot always been bare?

The bell tolls twelve. Centuries, hours.
The story's not new.
All that's left in the annals
is one undersize shoe.

The Mad Hatter dances and holds my hand,
drags me up and down a dreary chessboard land;
pawns to the left of me and pawns to the right,
pawns to the front and rear – and not a king in sight.

The Mad Hatter keeps on exchanging my hat:
I turn into Queen, Duchess, grinning Cheshire Cat.
"Please, I am Alice, Sir!" I try my best to scream,
but the hats keep flowing in an endless stream.

"A thousand hats or a thousand masks –
what might be the difference?" the Hatter asks.
"If the hats all fit, you get to wear them all,
be the Queen of all the pawns, and ten feet tall."

"I don't want the pawns, and the hats hurt my head;
the masks are too heavy – they weigh me down like lead;
since there's miles and miles of this black-and-white-
    checked sand,
there must be a King to rule this chessboard land!"

The Mad Hatter laughs: "Can't you see the light?
These fields have an end and there's a King, all right,
but you won't find him; and even if you do,
with all those hats about, he won't know it's you."

I doff all the hats, and politely I say:
"Thank you for the lesson, Sir! It's clear as day:
I must drop the masks, if I want to keep my name;
yes, I see the light, and I see through your game:

Both of us are gamesters, you no less than I;
you take off your hats, too, and look me in the eye:
guessed your game, I know your name, I'm taking your
    hand:
checkmate, your Majesty, great King of all this land!"

GRAIL KNIGHTS

In the morning when I wake up
I am always sure
that before I sleep again
I will have made the world
a better place to wake in
every following day.
My armour, laid
on the chair last night,
stands waiting, my sword –
the great white rose you brought me
from the market, when you went
out hunting yesterday –
beside the night-lamp,
ready to my hand.

I arm myself each morning
in the nodding horse-hair crest
of free will, and in the dreams of overnight
where little acts seemed glorious,
temptation just another dragon
and great acts possible.

You hold my hand as we walk to work
in pledge of the alliance
we made some years ago, together
to right the wrongs of every damsel
every child and every man
if we have to do it one by one
if we have to do it slowly
if we have to do it one day at a time.

Letter from a Minor Atlantic Auden

for Jeremy Brown

Just a short note of thanks for all your assistance,
and a humble request for a trifle more;
the day is not too far in the distance
when I know I'll be able to settle the score.
I'm writing more poems, of every description,
one to suit every subject or taste;
soon you'll be hard put to place a subscription
to any good monthly whose tone they don't raise.

Just try and laugh at my many rejections!
(and please pay my phone bill, or they'll cut it off);
you won't laugh when I dress you in Calvins,
feed you caviar and beef stroganoff;
when my London address is faber & faber,
jointly published by Random House;
when my copyright is by the *New Yorker*;
when we walk into Holt's, and not just to browse.

So what if the window is frozen shut solid,
that supper *chez moi* is always the same,
the carpet dingy, the kitchen sink squalid;
what's minor discomfort to eternal fame?
The cats may be thin, the cockroaches thinner,
and candle stumps no use against the cold,
but tomorrow's mail may produce a winner:
instead of SORRY, it may say SOLD.

My fiery lines will enkindle an uproar,
barely passing this side of the law;
why, I'm quite certain I'll be censored in Moscow,
and more than likely in Ontario.
My villa in Cannes, everyone's envy,
will be the very humblest of four;
my vineyards, endorsed by Lord Peter Wimsey,
turn out nothing but Chateau Latour.

So, please, regarding the abovementioned phone bill:
postpone your tuition, and buy off the wolf;
school yourself later. For now, there is baseball
on TV at home, and hockey or golf.
I, for my part, will *walk* to work. Briskly.
Stay off the Guinness, and get off the gin;
all forms of alcohol, 'cept Jameson's whiskey,
as an investment. Poets ought to be thin.

Les Fleurs Maladroites

One must always be drunk, said Baudelaire,
and he a poet everywhere admired,
as I should also like to be; so there
was every reason I, by him inspired,

began to write, and also took to drink.
Frequented public houses, pen in hand,
wrote even when I was too drunk to think
in rhyme or metre, or to understand

what I myself had set down on the sheet
of paper I would always carry 'round.
Always I hoped some publisher to meet,
who'd stopped to drink a pint while homeward bound;

but publishers do not frequent the same
saloons where I have made myself a name.

SNOW CROW

The snow lies over the riverbank
sparkling with a cold sense of humour
ill placed. A crow glares unblinking,
conspicuous; he is not laughing, does not
find it funny that he cannot find any
thing to eat under all this snow, and this
is mid-March. It ought to be easy, it ought
to be spring, his shabby black coat
not so glaringly obvious.

I look at him. We gongoozle a bit
at each other; look away, circle. We are
two of a kind, I think, you and I,
biding, just scraping by waiting for spring.
My black boots all salt-crusted, weather-stained,
like your draggled old coat, baggy crop. I say,
why not join forces, friend, how about it?
I can think of an act, a one-man-one-
crow thing, in which you perch
on my shoulder and harbinge away –
Odin's red-breasted raven – and I,
Odin himself-like, immortal, omnipotent or
nearly, and, topping all that, brother-in-law
to Freia the Young, Freia the Golden –
we'll show them, we'll show them all how
it may not be spring, but one man and one crow,
godlike in concert, can make it be so.

Wolf Dreams

There are recurrent animals.
Legendary, proverbial; animals of folklore.
No quarter, no mercy, don't blink;
stare down the barriers, pass through locked doors,
sink
in.
Wolves are like that.
Parallax creatures depending on angles
of view.
Beautiful; terrible; armies with banners
of Solomon's song.
Fear of the deepest I,
I dream of wolves.
Jungian solutions to Freudian dreams.
Girl dressed in scarlet, basket on forearm,
meeting the terror
of meeting
down some uncharted flesh-reeking maw,
taken and eaten
come true.
Girls who cry wolf have never been eaten.
There lies the stigma, the point.
I should know.

Tales of the Old World. Tales of the old wives
told under garlic, wolfsbane and rood.
Old tales, old wives.
In their way true.

The New World has legends and stories too.
The northern climes' younger, less cluttered memory,
larger and simpler,
less muddled
wolves.

Straightshooting, monogamous, not given to abstract
questions of philosophy; cut to the chase,
run silent, strike head-first like lightning
on snow. Almost an island,
a law
to himself that he cannot break
to another. Almost
a brother.
Creature of day stalking his shadow
in play,
creature of night howling his lovesong
to a mate
in the moon.

Staring and staring
straight laser eyes –
a hunter's, a shaman's –
read inbetween,
burn into depths
unseen, unspoken;
clean;
pass through locked doors,
stare down the barriers
across the divide
soul calls to soul.

I dream of wolves.
Do wolves dream of me?
Or at all?

I don't know.
I don't know.
I don't know.

Kladrius

for David, 19 April 2003

Snow disappears as sorcerers do – poof!
it is gone, there is nothing but sidewalk
clear and grey, it is spring.
The Kladrius perches outside the window,
looks fixedly inward. You,
pale and shimmering-hot with the flush
pneumonia brings – below, in the city,
trees bloom planted in asphalt – return
the steady gaze of the bird. The Kladrius'
eyes glaze, glow with the fever. Wings rise,
unfurl. The sun is white fire, the winged
shadow quarters its mirror. Your eyes
the clear grey of sidewalks. Eyes of a bird.

Parsifal Encounters the Grail on the 20th Floor

for David, St. Valentine's Day 2003

Down among grey concrete bunkers
we toil. No lilies grow here. We look,
but do not see, we ask no questions, do
unto others; we are deaf, dumb, and blind.
We were told we must eat, hence we kill;
and are never sated. Ears will not hear,
eyes will not see, hearts will not feel;
gravity rules us.

Fields such as these exist now only
between the firmaments, high above cities.
Here, out of reach, we toil not, nor spin.
In these floating gardens inhabited
by pilgrims of grace and gravity, you
alone see clearly. Your slow, wounded eyes
have seen such love, such beauty, a nerve
runs from each to your heart. What is
essential, Saint-Exupéry's fox has taught me,
is invisible to the eye.

What is the Grail, and whom does it serve?
What is the Blood, the elixir of life?
Your too-open eyes – even sleep cannot
close them – and exhaustion-blurred vision
give you the in-sight to ask. The Grail
serves Mankind. It confers the grace
to synthesize chlorophyll, and feed
on light; that we need not kill.

Blue Planet

Those dreams where I see it are not my own.
They belong to an angle not possible
from here; a picture taken some other place,
seen through the lens of some other race
whose dreams I dream. They see it. A lost
in space, desperate, gambling screwball,
smaller than theirs. Wobbling along, not even
perfectly round, somewhat eccentric with its
caved-in pate; unsound, like a windfall apple
the farmers discard on the umpire's call.

Pinpoints of nightshade-light scattered at random;
not a star, no celebrity; alone in the wide dark,
in the measureless silence. Those others, they're
larger, more powerful, steadier, run straighter,
shine simpler, some sashed in halo-like rings.
Attractively saturnine, gravity-conscious, serious
planets. Brown-grey – or is it the spectrum – or
yellow, sand-slate, even a martial red of a sort.
All earth-tones, the designers said.

And, think about it: vacant; dead. As far as we
know. This lopsided, fragile, off-balance bauble,
symphonied Gaia with a goddess's name
She Who Must Be Obeyed or else
this emerald space-isle, jewel-electron
of the nucleus star we hail as the Sun
is blue. She lives and lets live: the prime
directive's galactic blueprint; Captain Kirk;
Gandhi; Mother Teresa; Superman; Chief
Seattle; the Christ; the Buddha; hell, even Satan,
all said the same.

Sum up, ergo, and cogitate on these foreign
lapis lazuli dreams: *how can it be blue?*

Understand me; there is no other like it, at all.
This "it," it's alive, it's I and each other, we,
ours, and us, and you! Think, who'll not believe
in the miraculous: how . . . can it live . . . how
can it be . . . blue?

Brother to Dragons, Companion to Owls

for François Villon, George Faludy, and Patrick Henry

Give me circuses and give me bread,
let me play the wastrel grasshopper and never fear.
I shall but sleep according to how I make my bed
and find salvation sooner in the here
and now, below the starry sky, than any warm but cramped
abode with walls. I charge no-one with the burden of my soul:
I have yet to hear that Dante put a tramp
in his infernal circles. I am vagabond, but I am whole.
Let them all eat cake, and let me eat cake
too. Let me wear the world about me till it's thread-
bare. I know not what course others may take,
but as for me, give me circuses and give me bread.

My father was a shepherd, beloved of the mad god
who breathes fire into wine and poets. As a boy
he tended goats in Arcadie. His lord
was Pan himself, who gave him for a toy
his set of pipes, to take his stance
upon the green Arcadian hills and play. Together
they taught the goats to dance;
gods, goats, mortals – all birds of a feather –
dancing the nights away. They taught me, too, to make
anything with feet to dance today, and never dread
tomorrow. I know not what course others may take,
but as for me, give me circuses and give me bread.

My mother is the green earth, Gaia of the apples
and of quetzal feathers in her hair,
Gaia of the horses and of dappled
deer, Gaia young, immense, marvellous, and bare-
breasted, intoxicated all the day upon her cow-
slip wine. My tail is plaited like a Barbary ram,
I am as handsome as biblical lilies, and how,
indeed, should I not be, taking after my dam?

My sire was playing for very high stakes
on Pan's pipes for *her* to dance to, to turn her head.
Shall I do less? I know not what course others may take,
but as for me, give me circuses and give me bread.

I leave no name behind me when I go,
nor do I know if I go anywhere at all,
but while I am here the only law I know
is the one the grey wolf lives by: I call
only what my two hands can defend my own,
and give half of that to him who needs it when we meet;
call the place I sleep this night my home,
and when I move on be sure I did not keep
in my possession anything to make
my footsteps heavy where I tread
upon my Mother. I know not what course others may take,
but as for me, give me circuses and give me bread.

I may go somewhere even better hence, or I may not;
but one thing I know: I like it here, this gift
of all this life and air my father gave to me, and got
from his, and so forth. To be sure that I had lived
and breathed as much of it as one man can
by rights, and that I gave the moon something to look
at every night, and that I did not give the sun
much cause for boredom watching as he took
his daily course above me east to west, I make
my sole concern. Come with me, if you would be fed
properly for once, my lords. I know not what course
        others may take,
but as for me, give me circuses and give me bread.

NOTES

"**Metropolis**" – "Clepsydra:" A water-clock. Not unlike an hourglass. Water drips into a floating bowl which eventually sinks in a predetermined period of time.

"**Icarus**" – "AGO" – The Art Gallery of Ontario.

"**Woman as Mountain**" – Inspired by a painting by Toronto artist Elizabeth Greisman.

"**Pietá**" – Inspired by the poem "Gabriel, Descending" by Jean Hull Herman.

"**Chi: Blood and Earth (Mishima Yukio)**" – Inspired by a brush painting by American artist James Birthrong which suggests the "chi" character of the Japanese hiragana syllabary, and resembles a kneeling man with his arms thrown wide. The "chi" character can be read as "blood," as "earth," and as "mind."

"**The Puppet Master**," "**The Prince's Ball**," and "**Worship**" – All were inspired by brush paintings by James Birthrong.

"**I, Ahab**" – "Dismembered'immolay:" Jacques de Molay, Grand Master of the Knights Templar, tortured and burned at the stake in 1314, following the suppression of the order. Several of the references in this passage are to the Knights Templar and their successors, the Freemasons. "Nommo:" Equivalent to the Sumerian and Babylonian tradition of Oannes, the Nommo are a legendary amphibian race, half fish, half man, depicted in Assyrian temple carvings. They travelled the universe and made a civilization on Earth. See R.K.G. Temple, *The Sirius Mystery*, and the story of Noah in Genesis 8: 15-19, source of mermaid legends.

"**Judas' Dream**" – "Poppy and memory" – is from Paul Celan, as too in "Ahab Asleep – in Ophelia's Garden".

"**Whales Weep Not**" – The title is taken from D.H. Lawrence's poem.

"**Ahab Asleep**" – In the geocentric world of the ancient Egyptians, the dead travelled towards resurrection by the path the sun took under the earth when it set in the west, to rise again in the east. Before burial, a ceremony known as the "opening of the mouth" took place, wherein the priest symbolically opened the mouth of the mummy with a small blade-like instrument, so as to enable him to answer in the Underworld for his deeds. Mummies that underwent this ritual were effectively transformed into vessels for the Ka (life-force, soul) of the deceased. Upon arrival there, the Ka was first confronted by Anubis, guardian of the Underworld, and Maat, goddess of Truth, and his heart was weighed in a pair of scales against a feather, symbol of Maat.

"**Akhenaten**" – According to Immanuel Velikovsky, the origins of the Oedipus legend are to be sought in the life and character of Egypt's historical Akhenaten, pharaoh of the 18th dynasty of the New Kingdom. His unorthodoxy, his worship of the sun-disc Aten in his own peculiar way, and the physical oddities that made their way into the art of the period as the celebrated Amarna Style, have earned him, among other associations, the epithets "heretic" and "the first monotheist," as well as the unremitting interest of posterity. "*Non omnis moriar*" – "I shall not altogether die" – is from Horace, *Odes*, III, xxx, 6.

"**Kladrius**" – Var. *caladrius*: mythical bird. It was believed in the Middle Ages that a sick man whose illness was not terminal could return the steady gaze of the bird; having absorbed the disease, the bird was then said to fly up to the sun and disperse the disease. See E. A. Armstrong, *The Life and Lore of the Bird*.

"**Parsifal Encounters the Grail on the 20th Floor**" – Lines 7 and 8 of stanza 2 are paraphrased from Milton Acorn's poem "If You're Stronghearted;" chlorophyll synthesis for humans as a means of feeding on light is from Simone Weil, *Gravity and Grace*.

"**Brother to Dragons, Companion to Owls**" – The title is taken from Job 30: 29.

Acknowledgements

Many of the poems in this book, or earlier versions of them, appeared in the following publications: *Dream International Quarterly, Möbius, Pablo Lennis, Psychopoetica, The Brobdingnagian Times, Blind Man's Rainbow;* the anthologies *The Frost Place Anthology of Participant Readings, Beyond These Charted Realms, In Quest of the Miracle Stag, The Incredible Journey of the Instant Anthology;* two chapbooks by Fooliar Press; and several anthologies of the *National Library of Poetry*. Thanks to each of their editors. Radio shows: *Gaywire Live* and *Howl* (CIUT). Reading series: Poetica, The Art Bar, The Idler, I.V. Lounge, CoffeeHouse Cabaret, The Arts and Letters Club's Red Salon, Syntactic Sunday, Words Aloud, Bite, and Pitbull. Thanks to each of their hosts. Special events: the Gwendolyn MacEwen Memorial readings at the Pteros Gallery, Poem for Peace in Many Voices, La Sirena. Thanks to each of their hosts and organizers. Thanks also to all members of Flight, Muse Co-op, the Vic Group, and the Art Bar Group, past and present.

A copy of this book is hereby sent into spirit, as promised, for Peter W. Prole, and for Jeremy Brown, *quibus sine forsan non.*

I am deeply grateful to all who have offered encouragement and support for my writing and other literary activities throughout.

More than thanks are due to:

Allan Briesmaster, my editor and friend, for his vision and patience.

My parents, Zsuzsa and Laszlo Jarmai, for the world, in both fact and metaphor.

My brother, Tom Jarmai, who has always said what he meant and meant what he said; for everything, always.

David Newel for all his faith, love, and help in this as in everything, and for bringing me the Grail.

And You.